fever

fever

Leanne Averbach

Mansfield Press

Library and Archives Canada Cataloguing in Publication

Averbach, Leanne
        Fever / Leanne Averbach.

Poems.
ISBN 1-894469-23-2

        I. Title.

PS8601.V46F49 2005   C811'.6   C2005-901925-5

Acknowledgements: *The Birds of Sarajevo*, Grain Magazine, 2003; *Stoplight*,
Washington Square, New York City, 2003; *Fiftieth Wedding Anniversary*,
Pottersfield Portfolio, 2003; *Dining with Family, Deathwatcher*, Wayne
County Review, Newark, NY, 2003; *Moment, Willow*, Descant, 2003;
Beneath, Big City Lit International Chapbook Contest, Honourable Mention,
New York City, 2003; *Opening*, Poetry In Performance #30, City College,
New York City, 2002; *Aisle of Hope*, Ripple Effect Press, Love in the Media
Age Anthology, 2001; *Ivy*, (previously entitled *"blue moon over forever"*) and
The Funeral, The Fiddlehead, 2000; *Grandfather's Hand*, Canadian Women's
Studies, 2000; *By the Sea*, The Landmarks 2000 Project; *Abattoir*, (previously
entitled *"Kill Floor 1974"*) Sub-TERRAIN runner-up in Last Poems Poetry
Contest, 2000; *Popping Herring Roe*, Event, 1999; *After the Storm, Almost
Was*, The New Quarterly, 1999; *The Gift, Reading the Signs*, Dalhousie
Review, 1999; *Carwash*, Antigonish Review, 1999; *Funeral Fictions*, Poetry
New Zealand, 1999; *Bird, Is Just a Kiss*, Descant, 1998; *Memories Don't*,
Sub-TERRAIN, 1996

Design: Denis De Klerck, Rick O'Brien, Marijke Friesen
Cover Art: Bonnie Leyton
The publication of *Fever*
has been generously supported by
The Canada Council for the Arts and
The Ontario Arts Council.

Mansfield Press Inc.
25 Mansfield Avenue, Toronto, Ontario, Canada. M6J 2A9
Publisher: Denis De Klerck
www.mansfieldpress.net

We have art in order to not die of the truth
Friedrich Nietzsche

To my father, a man of few words,
and to my mother who taught me to love them.

CONTENTS

One

Two

Three

One

Born This Way

Hair of four colours,
a fetching freak at birth.
Gray makes five.

My mother, accused, snarled
Born that way, hair and all!
and they shut up, disbelieving.
I grew accustomed.

Always had a wild taste; the sea, never far.
A span of attention short and forgiving
as a Newfoundland summer.
Capsicum addict, food ruby hot.
My lips, wandering and fleeing,
learned from my ancestors.
Language my demiurge.
Intolerant: of ideology, people
arranged in circles,
intolerance.
Apostate, actor, bumbler, recluse.
Gray makes five.

Fire in my mouth,
Russian steppes in my blood.
Lips that live.

Memories Don't

Memories don't space travel
no.

These psychic cosmonauts
bore inward through the nape
where a kiss has been mislaid

or down the throat
delivered in the sidecar
of a bitter remark.

Then they swim
like Mao against the tide
or march
like Gandhi to the sea
irresistibly
through the marrow of years

until they soak into the bloodstream
and raft northward on the flow
to arrive uninvited
on some cerebral coil
there to play hide and seek
indefinitely.

No
unlike ghosts
who are rather civilized
visiting, inhabiting houses
like you and me

memories are quite insane;

that's why they travel
only in the brain.

especially since dad
was a pedlar boy
wending his way through
stiff Canadian streets
hawking newspapers, berries, childhood
returning home to soup and silence

a self for making
only into a man
to whom little is said today
save bounced off a gargantuan screen
towards which he is couched
(and a fabulous couch it is)

frowning and wondering
how one life of strife
bred such a sloth
as me

GRANDFATHER'S HAND

I don't remember the time
not yet four
I climbed into his cool lap, guided
by that ringed hand like gold tongs
missing the trigger finger – the least he could give
to dodge Russian wars – and his gray eyes
rolled high up, proud, into his hairless
onion head, his great gold-filled mouth opening too wide
as he bragged my heart's desire was
                              a Cadillac.

Though it was a *catalogue* I'd yearned for – the rich
candy-coloured gloss of the Hudson's Bay annual –
the joy his error gave him so filled the room that day
it became family lore, close to a memory
of the old cold man who wore spats in the old country
and a swaggering fist in the new
leaving this, The Cadillac Legend, for my moral
                              direction.

How I failed him. My dreams of driving
injustice into the sea not *his* idea. A woman without
a tea set, unstudied in the sequined arts, the hair salon.
Now this penniless scribbling:

a bird in the grass
or the magnificent scent
of a lover's groin uncoiling
enough to drive me to a page, consider
the unforeseen traffic of our lives.

Annual Dine with Family

It's tradition. Our lives, soft but firm
as jelly molds, are carved wide
open, and the earnest scab of a year's forgetting
is picked off like unwanted pie crust.
Clamped around the biggest table,
a noisy bloodless slaughter.

The present gongs with repetitions.
Stories spill like gene pools across
pink wine ghosts in the tablecloth.
The eyes of the very young
roll and roll, feeling as yet
only boredom. But the cruel drone
of the unforgiving
hums right along like a longlife bulb
on its last legs. Though we have all
overeaten, some, the usual victims, are
shrunken and pale:
now inert as the whitefish quills
decorating the last platters.

I tell myself what I need
is a breather, more therapy perhaps,
and the ordeal will lift
rising like sweet meringue.
These are after all
mere people; the door, vibrating
at me now at the end
of the photo-choked hallway,
just a door.

Is Just a Kiss

In the dream the dog's tongue
poured into your widening mouth and

I inquired as to your pride;
you reminded me good taste

derives from variety and
besides, you had fallen in love

with the moment.
The dog, whose name I have suppressed,

heaved her happiness
as began the next episode:

my father dying in hospital
his dogged sourness

sweetening towards oblivion.
Parting, my lips spoke your name and

instantly there, you guided me
toward your gigantic tongue:

all my ducts spilt
at your largesse

and I awoke
fully lit.

THE FUNERAL

At 87, her bones were as light as pencils.
Her daughter, almost erased from years of servitude,
watches the shovel count off her own time left.
The young rabbi calls her loyal, calls her Shirley
instead of Sherry – his first funeral.
Rain blows hard across the field of stones,
umbrellas aching to snap. The family plot:
six spots left. Shoes sink into the waiting
ground and rhythmic prayers fill us with
secular shame. She was a cruel woman.
Still we came, felt our ancestors pull
at the hems of our overcoats.

By Metrotown Station, I Sat Down & Wept

I step from the platform, take a seat with the other possessed.

I have left my father's decaying bedside for the night.
Boxes of world flicker past and I reach inside
like my hands in his pockets in the closet searching for change.

I know he is no policeman. Since the *shtetl*
fear and money have risen
beneath him like a pot of porridge, out of control
and never enough. They ooze through his mouth
as if scorched by the journey. How can he help it:
pain makes us all rage in the key of F.

Here are my memories.
Once his huge agate ring
slid forever into the blue wash of a Hawaiian beach
and I found it, returned it to that hand.
His smile soaked into my red braids, then it kissed me
with a brag to his friends.

He would watch me swim laps by the hundreds,
count them off like husbands in waiting. To teach me
humility, he would stand me next to my beautiful mother.
Once, driving a friend and me somewhere
he sang This Old Man with us so many times,
my friend looked at him like a father.

Daddy provided steak and sequins;
the rest was up to me.
The years crept past like little criminals,
unapprehended.

FIFTIETH WEDDING ANNIVERSARY

My big cousin the shrink
from L.A.
who tried to deflower me as part of his internship
was there,
as was his mother the dowager
wielding her double canes.
Always nuts Aunt Rose arrived but now
just hiding her clothes and forgetting
to inquire about my promiscuity or prescribe
technicolour diet pills.
The long long tresses of my brilliant nephew who
the night before had fucked a girl on my brother's fabulous lawn
came from Montreal,
causing a few canes to wag.
That Marilyn Munroe ringer aunt
the one who went after my baby cousin, now obese,
with a cleaver for stealing a candy from a drawer
showed up.
And my favourite cousins,
the ones who helped me, age eleven, find my clit
came
with their lovely wives.

Master of Ceremonies was my brother.
For years he assiduously
screwed the maids but now
made an impression
when he got up to deliver a speech
and upturned the head table;
the video crew he had paid for
caught it all.

Mom and dad cringed,
shame confusing the joy
they had never quite known
during fifty years,
not since the good times: a week
of unforbidden honeymoon sex.
The rest
said my mom
she'd rather just forget.

WILLOW

The willow spills soft margins onto a platter
of earth: this, our measure of earth, my children's and mine.

From my window I look down upon it and a raven
pacing over boughs, cawing to the sun, rip click ripping the air

with mischief dry and brittle. This is the sound
of disappointments. It all sends me down

stairs, and still I hear the black bird.
Yet, the willow. See its cool emerald mane

across this path I must travel
to our door: knobby bones of branch

that clack
in the wind like a beaded curtain

signifying transgression, escape
from things, longing, my face

where once glassy pools of I reflected any
you. Now splintered with brackish tributaries

of doubt, willfulness, an evil eye for inanity. Yet on my face
too is evidence of dreams

their imprecision restoring sensation
of doorways. Last night I dreamed my father died

happily; I played classical notes in his Frank Sinatra ear
and he smiled, proud I had invented something new, lucrative.

The Man Who Mistook His Daughter for a Sheet

The first thing you'd see, those blue pools of eye.
Next, the sad feet, like horns
of a bull bowed over the brave

defeated man. Yes, let's imagine the ring, the barbaric
contest between man and animal.
The man, my father; the animal, my father.

For nearly a century he regaled the crowds
with salesmanship. He is the devil
who once, as you admired the brocade skirt

on a sofa would sell you the shirt
off your back, and the sofa too and an icebox
to keep the free gallon of ice cream and your heart

racing after the sudden
sale. Then he was talking into a
hospital sheet where my voice appeared

to call him on the phone.
Such a flim-flam thank-you m'am
man, now my old man

is gone. The rich patternless
bruises decorating his limbs
like the torn coat of the toreador

gone too, cowed, caged, boxed
and delivered, the usual deal – a lifetime
guarantee, expired.

EULOGY

Unexpected, the coffin
more like a contraption, a crate
for home delivery.
The Jews, ordinarily more
ornate, keep it simple
here. It was unexpected
looking down at him, the crated,
then out to the gathered, naked
in their confused pieces.
Only the oldest versed in how, this.
Some faces like rain
others cellophaned inside
estimating their scars,
coming up with breath
still in their lungs.
Of him I spoke.
I a great insectivore daughter
echolocating through his dark.

Two

THE BIRDS OF SARAJEVO

Sunday morning we heard more war
in the distance, and soon
the rain was falling like slag
murdering the crocuses.

This from my friend
in her elegant hand.

Her words pull
across the page and down,
a single sinew
weighted at its end . . .

The news of war Sunday morning
was a language ancient
as stones and fire, constituents
of the everyday.

But we are, if nothing else,
inventive when it comes to finding
an hour for making love; chaos spoils
otherwise. We loved as usual.

On her visits here to the staggering calm
of Canada, we will push our work papers aside
and replenish our glasses with the Balkans,
speak of how strange
love's fragile mouth like a river mouth
can still open inside war
        to the taste of the sea.

Our roof was quiet above us
on Sunday as we curved, one
inside the other, in our warm
afternoon attic.

Then a thrashing rain descended;
it was just past noon.

Out our window
someone cried
          "A child has fallen!"
Shot like a bird
from a courtyard birch,
a sprig of buds bleeding in her hand.

And here – see her words
press, a backward slant
into the thin blue pulp,
like nails curled back
into their own flesh.

Our neighbour's child.
Rain sinking into the mud around her
like tiny missiles;
and that damned tree still standing,
grotesquely beginning its year.

Another child, just a line
in the poetry of our mad warriors.

We loved as usual; the rain has stopped
for now.

IN LIEU OF TREES
(from Columbus Circle, New York City—the view)

March pumps sideways
from Con Edison stacks. They shove
their hard snapped-on moods into wind spent
across puckered suburban shores, houses
and housewives considering: themselves, the batter
of winter, how another season. Women
examining: their peeling Martha walls, and their renovated
friends who gloat winter was *not* wasted –
as if breath and flesh were cheap utilities.

Soon numbered young will carry heads
home under their arms, throw and hoop them,
and the world will sleep some more.
But for now, the gashes of smoke die of cold
exhaustion and the bridges sway in lieu of trees or Ray Charles
or twin towers, their remnants rattling in the pockets of men
with an eye for collectibles.

THE VIEW
(Gulf War Memory,'92)

I am
streaked with pallid TV light

over there
a chair
cat full & leering

the air is
thin with neglect
only cat breath to drive it

it went on weeks like that
entombed in that room
the hum of events gently
whirring
like a box of fireflies

countless suns arching
beautifully falling

sanguine
as a general
silent as corpses
melting

until the menace of peace
descended

dreamily as a sandstorm
in a paperweight

we were always in such a hurry
then, the imminence of revolution
swaddling us like hairshirts

and the nights too
after the day's hard verdicts
were held between the gray sheets
of our sunless bodies
like dangerous theories, things
too private to be our property

but too explosive to contain
so we made two sons
who troll other continents now
for ineffables—things
that go wow in the night

Ivy

Three weeks in Okalla prison, Chairman Mao proud
of me I think, shaking like a paddywagon,

trying to remember his round buffed face, a cherub
with ambition, as I pasted his poster image

over a grimy telephone pole just before
being jumped and arrested, slogans

pounding up arteries and way out
of my pink ideological throat.

And now I am learning about Ivy, a 60-year-old
junked out bag lady, in here for rolling a non-civilian,

though it all started when she was 14, snatched a warm gun
from a cop's burnished hip.

The same gun, the officer had said
to Ivy and her mother in the kitchen

(and here she shows me
how he slapped his blackhide holster

with John Wayne delectation) the same one he'd used to shoot
her big brother, out stealing cars in Burnaby

for fun that Saturday night, blue moon rising over
Forest Lawn cemetery, cool and steady as a black and white

sedan, as a pallid TV moon, shot him dead, that same moon pouring
glow over the crusted docks where Ivy's dad worked

and took, sold then drank whatever
the long shore allowed

The heavy revolver, unmanageable as her mother's
face, slipped from Ivy's small fingers

and her fingerprints, like little shadow puppets on the wall
of the rest of her life, sent her here and there and now here

with me, a kid with my copy of Lenin's *What Is To Be Done?*
stuffed and dampening in my speechless fist.

RIO DE JANEIRO
January 2003

The night is upon me, drink
bowling through the portents of war, the stern pins
of my convictions upended and slain

I think: as if that
were not enough,
this sticky heat   It leans

With me out into a throat
of inner courtyard, my eyes
taking in the unshuttered narratives

Three walls of them and
the moon above full
of accusation   But these lives

Flung wide   tongues
of cotton whorling chairs,
limbs, like the muscular

Sails of Portuguese caravels
coloured wild with yearning
for land, now limp and awash

In the blue glow
of television   Television: the poor man's puppy
at the foot of every bed, every bed

As still-waiting as ours for news; the Rio heat
cloying and hungry   the thrum rising
now from the streets of wakened

Night feet, the poorest coming
down the moonlit hips of shanty
hills – swaying and hopeless and joyful

SIZE

"... is an arguable defence."

Jean Chrétien, on hemispheric economic blocks after
the 1997 Vancouver APEC Conference

Tight rows of limousines
leer down the rain-buffed West Coast avenues,
a one-way look in their windows.
Tonight, the Asia-Pacific has come to dine
        in my home town.

Eighteen heads
of state, "blocked" like a vast sweater
being brought under control.
Like currencies they rise from their limousines,
cameras frothing. And later in the pastel hall, diners swap jokes
        about the protests outside.

"This drizzle," carps Indonesia's Suharto.

And to put him in better humour
the President proposes a toast
and seventeen heads bob
from their matching Canadian cowhide jackets.

Size, you see, is the arguable defence.
Outside, protesters set up little tents.

In the Naval Museum, Venice

In the 16th century this is how
in order to incite luck in war
the fleet was wed to the sea:
a huge jewel-studded ring
was strapped tight to the woman
adorning the prowhead, and after she fell heavy
into god's foaming arms, men in dry suits
plunged deep beneath
to unfasten the ring,
bring it home.

Now the hoops of love
lie alone in gilded boxes.
And the prows with their big maidens
still attached fill the sumptuous enormity
of Venetian room after room. Vast
as mastidons, they are trapped
in this hubris interval with man.
Nearby sabers and cannons,
mannequins in tranquil
readiness: tractable, metal, masculine.
Plumes, leathers and epaulets,
a *haute couture* timeline of war
stretching out to sea
where a president is made
luminous in a flight suit.
Battle chic: it gets away with murder.

MOMENT

Our winter sea rolls in
thick as green-black jam.
Like the quiet inside
this room we built
heavy with everything
we have and do not want.
A conch on the endtable
like a severed ear
plugged with cigarette ends
is spared the sound
of our stillness.

I cannot take my eyes
off your wrists. The way
the moody hairs bluster
from your cuffs. I would
stroke them, feel under your
clothes that way in public;
now, just sad places one part
of you joins another.

The daily news is that blood
wars are out of hand,
and the climate loves
to devastate the poor.
I would like to add
that the sea is thickening
and tight fists of cloud
are taking aim overhead.

I could leave at dawn, run
to Prague or Budapest
to weep with the veterans of gloom.
But I will stay awhile, inhale
beside you this slow
sickening moment.

Funeral Fictions

The priest today with his wafers, scentless
Incense, and his wine iced by the air

Wants us all to believe
It was Jesus just died, not our Da.

A guitar player strums, two singers sing
Soporific numbers, and sorrow

Wonders at how even the twelve waxen apostles
Encircling high above the pulpit

Seem ready to drift off, fall
Onto the plastic pillars, flowers, the immaculate

Sears carpeting, the sleepy
Altar boys. Wonders

If Grandad in the coffin, at rest
Now in his Sunday cathedral culture

Loved this blandness
The way I love Leonard Cohen

Or the Lambada.
Or did he suffer from a hellish craving

To use his wit on a nightclub stage
Kiss the feet of a diva

Or apply that heart that finally failed him
To run far away

From this flat world, sail a schooner
to Tahiti

Take up with a brown woman, browner
Than any single face

Gathered here today in this milky
Hall, where those of us who

Loved him struggle to
Feel him gone.

POPPING HERRING ROE

smocked and hair-netted
we sidle up to the trough
unprepared for this:

from the basin flow
our rubber claws must pluck out
the females one-by-one

while the males
are left, carried to a simple
mass grave

once in hand
the procedure is quick
as a pop

as one hand
holds her,
belly-up

while the other
springs a thumb
like a blade

enter and thrust
enter and thrust
and the stream fills

with afterlives,
small translucent sacs of luxury
destined to cross the Pacific once more

in a jar;
the scales of their mothers
and fathers, their great sea stench

left behind
in our hair, under our skin,
in our beds at night

and on the bus ride home
the space the other riders make
between themselves

and us
reminds us of
what we have done

ABATTOIR

From somewhere over there
the monotonous people-screams
of pigs are cut with pops
innocent as firecrackers.
Nothing much
from the cows, the stoics,
who swallow their fear
with soft oboe moans.

I've been sent to the Kill Floor
for a special task. 10,000 sealed packs of bologna
forgotten and spoiled. A few of us are chosen,
assigned to crouch around The Pit
and empty the units of meat
one-by-creamy-one; but after an hour,
only two of us have not run off
to empty ourselves.

The stench, having nowhere to go, crawls
into my mouth, while my eyes and ears
get busy arguing ontology. Without their hair
save a few sprigs missed by the flame gun
animals have no race; beneath their browns
reds and calicos, they are all plain as white men,
severely deformed white men: best to eat them.

The freshly deceased.
Slung cheek to cheek they
glide overhead on hooked tracks.
Spilling onto the beetle heads of men.

My meatmate and I work silently
avoid the hazards of open mouths
toss the rotten meat into the hole
for dog food, fertilizer.

Across the gorge a face
beneath a hair net, the rubbery surface of her skin
now thick with the oily atmosphere and that hardhat
spilling red from above and down her neck
like mine.

The woman on the other side
works out the day with me, until at last:
the sudden, boorish beauty of the horn whistle.

It urges us to the exit.
The bang of the card clock
triggers talk about the blueglow and beer to come
as hardhats and smocks
purple from brush strokes with flesh
weave out through the less soiled
incoming shift.

BY THE SEA

Beneath a pin-striped umbrella
a blanket hysterically coloured
and a brunette with a book

Gulls rise and fall on soft
marble clouds reflected in the sea
sunburned hills behind

An infant flies
his sea-wet flesh glistening
back down into his father's arms

and a lifeguard is rowing tight circles
around nothing or someone
his blind chair watching

while a large family discusses the beach
they left behind, another ocean
and the shells of relatives

Over there, cheering volleyballers
oblivious to the homesick rocking
of freighters, let alone to other shores

And thirty years ago
your hot silhouette, my high
salt-stained boots

and the paisley twirl of my skirt
rolled with you into the applause
of this very sea

The book is not about this
the lifeguard, just a man, prefers blondes
It is raining in Santiago

THE DARE

The chill-splintered voices of children
in the gully fly up to the one high on the bridge,
goading her off.

Chicken! Chicken! they shout
        like gulls screaming at trash.

Funny, she thinks as she steps
out into glory, there above the surging glacial melt,
the darelit afternoon. The wind running
through the ravine, ready to spread the news.
Gray boulders whitesilvering below
        with river foam, roaring like God

does at home before the lights go
out and she divides into two
for her father, leaving her mind behind.

He is slung now in the lazy-boy
and waiting, foam on his prickly
quiet. No matter. Mothers
all the way to Toronto
        will read about her tomorrow.

SHE'S A PEACH

As if he had stolen her nose.

With her popped-in eyes
and collapsible ears,
she's a peach, a melonhead.

Today, each day, it was
home from work to cook,
cook him quiet, quiet and still,
dead and tired, that's what she likes
to hear, to think: tonight will be quiet

as lamps and ashtrays
that have forgotten how to fly.

Funny how she knows though
the moment she arrives
into the hard TV blue
a few reckless moments late
now dirty with memories
of her future.

Perhaps it's his eyes
cold burning through the back
of his oily skull
or the aluminum cans
slain at his side,
their Münch-mouths wailing:
where were you
where the hell

So now her nose is gone,
her ears are split pomegranate
halves, and the shelves of her eyes
are white and bare,
doorless as her sealed lips.

DEATHWATCHER
for G.B.

Sometimes I dream this for you
in place of your suicide:

stratus gathering
to catch your fall like a lucky mitt
or my arms.

For you who ministered so many men
into the ethers past hell.

I give this to you
in place of the oil-filthed sea.
The cold roil of October
beneath the rigid cable span
of that bridge
pulling your never fierce face
down, down past the stiff girders
watching you like so many laid out men.

We studied together, you and I, pinned
in miserable student seats, how Picasso
refused *Guernica* to The Party.
We swooned at the bastard's wisdom
to defend death from the spectacle of ideology.

We are not meant to be deathwatchers.

You ministered many men into oblivions.
Gorgeous states where
                a virus is no more
forbidding than a preference, or the common autumn
                trees disrobing.

BONE AND BRUSH
to artist Bonnie Leyton, my sister, in Rwanda, 1995

I've seen it,
people brushing up against you
succumbing to angels.
You have always worn the truth
of things like a wide milk mustache.
The hilarious absurd. Everyone
wanting to kiss it off you.

But it is you
that has just come from Rwanda
back home to Paradise, Newfoundland.
And you are being followed.

Rows upon parched rows of bone people
their eyes opaque-hard as bergs
floating across the Rwandan hills
out of the Great Rift Valley
on a narrow dust sea
marching from enemy to enemy
only the sound of bone lifting cotton
and dust climbing
through so many shoes, so many shoes.

No child left
in the children marching there;
only stale dust rising past long elegant fibulae
past femurs, up into vulvae curling
them dry as wild berry leaves, dust caking
phalluses into stiff arrows
of hatred, even the ones who had not murdered
much yet.

Your soft wide eyes felt the dry
shock of a church of skulls
a warm wind eddying around neat rows

into their sockets accented with machete blades
little bullet holes gently whistling.

And you could have thought then
of those who shoot
at fish in ponds. But all thought
had fled, feelings shoved into the rafters of your
nightmares which do not begin for weeks
until you are home again
with the Atlantic, your easel,
your wailing clay-stained hands –
then they never end.

Hard what you saw, sister, how more
than any of it I feared for myself
losing you.

Phone Call Home
for my son, James

You were born into a marriage of storms
in basements. Teacups of gray
sleepless years, nights split with
polemics, the grind of the press
marching into mornings, jail cells,
meetings about meetings,
an infinite array
            of fanatical rites.

I brought you unplanned
into all this
out of me and into red
walls peeling slogans –
the resuscitated drapery
of a century exhausted,
heavy with signs
that all the gods were dead.
But I soldiered on.

And I wonder, did you feel it,
all that ideology –
religion's homelier twin?

Two months early
you arrived pink, orange-haired,
an obvious clash
with all that red.

It was you
who first taught me
– vain with icons and gone strange
to the contours of my own
interior – how to love.

Today you phoned
home, you
are sturdy and quick and
orange-haired still
and carrying the traces of all
that sound and fury
which more than any of it
I had not planned.

You carry your world
the worlds you think
came before
stiff and clenched
afraid to let us down.

Let me tell you what I know:

that duty is guilt
and ends badly,

like ideology, the cold mortar
of innocence without mystery,
it makes you soft, then
it makes you hard.

And time is indifferent
to intention. It just spills.

Its best parts
have no names.

Only love can beguile it.

Three

I Dreamt of a Wood Fence

I dreamt of a wood fence, a hole
in it for viewing.
At first all I dared was to angle, examine
the hole itself. Its shallow throat
coated with sticky red resin, like a first show
of woman. My heart jigged. Tempted me
to withdraw from the aperture
back to a moment when fear was
away, tossing someone
else's brain into discord. But looking:
it was all there was.

Reclining in a slatted divan
too large for her doughy form
an infant gazed back into the hole
that was me. As if waiting long for my eyes
and their dark dilating yolks.
Her skin was glossy, plastic
as an old photograph.
Though she was emitting the sound of pink
melons falling fast to earth, my compulsion
to rescue froze inchoate. I could never
get to her in time.

In my morning
a scarp of dawn electrifies
a pomelo wedge
full glimmer in my spoon:
it is the dream remembered.

BIRTHDAY WISHES IN THE MIRROR

– Forty-nine –
your age hangs over you
like a recent death,
and your mirrors
are draped in your misery.
That tsunami
of dread swelling in your brow
has me worried,
and your pallor has turned a shade
of asylum green.

What of it, you are no longer
young?

Yesterday you saw the sky crack
open, out fell a bird
you could not name.
From the flesh of a pine tree
it withdrew a beetle and
then, casting its vitreous eye at you,
climbed into the sky again.

All that
in the crisp space between two skies.
Living, isn't it for this?

Consider then
your sons, their sudden confidences,
those large unaccusing hands.
Your sister's voice folding light
sibilants, her sculpture
of fruit eager as schoolgirls unpeeling.
Consider love, its unlocked cell.
This line born from distinct
nowhere. The constant stroking
of the moonstruck sea.

Two Older Dames Compare Tattoos

Delicate crane
green and yellow
elegant bird of hope
on your arm
now
a slack
and split open
banana peel.

My proud sun
with its crisp
corona of flames
abandoned on the moonscape
of my thigh
now a campfire
running low on wood.

As they mature, tattoos
soak in
to old skin
toward the core
where the woman is.

ALMOST WAS

As a child too I was short
on poise, and rarely silent.
But I loved my own sound
arriving, pressing like my angora

into womanhood. Loved to sing
even badly, practicing often
on strangers, phone book men,
with my breathiest 13-year-old coos.

Once, in Bardot purrs, I arranged a meeting
downtown, I would bring mother's poodle, Pierre,
and the man, he would carry beneath his coat
a long, dark *parapluie* to kiss me under.

But I reaped all my pleasure
beneath a tent of dark blankets
in a basement confession
steaming with girlish heat, frothing
and shrieking over
              what almost was.

So delicious, so
never-never, so all
there has ever been.

I still can't get over it.

WORKING WITH MY FAVORITE MISTER
for Noah Webster

You are on my lap, the temperature of leather.
Spread open and even like an animal across me.
Big and comprehensive; comfortable.
You gaze unabridged upwards: *trope, troth, Trotsky,*
troubadour, trousers, trout. Titillating.

Titillating troubling *trout.*
Wriggling to life: rainbow, cutthroat, brown and brook *Salmonidae.*
The facts swim in my sudden freshwater. Then
my truant hand, your copious lingua eyes, those oilskin haunches
which curve
into your powerful spine, oh.

Noah, between the two of us, the boat
may *never* get built!

ODE TO THE HOT PEPPER

Blackflies are wicked today,
could flay the mange off a cur.
That's not dust on the road;
flies brought relatives.
Must be as inbred as hillfolk,
way they chase each other
onto the coffee shop pane
or into the slack jaw of Simone
the fortune-teller.

Everyone's dreaming of cool;
icebergs of Labrador, maybe.
Can't think a thing. But,
that pepper plant over there,
one on the sill behind Frank,
reminds me of paradise.
Thick wet strokes
of paintings of paradise.

I'd love to paint it, strange thing,
so lovely even in this heat

waxy cocky buds
promise of fire
swimming in a grateful mouth.

Why, even the blackfly
would howl appreciation at
feeling so much so long so hard
in one place.

SWOON

He held my child throat
for me with his man's hand, showed me
how to find the throb
has its limits if he persisted, and later
a masturbatory swoon the result.
He meant it
as a game, nothing;
it became everything.
My psycho-sexual predicament
ever seeking the swoonmaker's twin.

INTERNET DATING

You can't imagine, all the street men
or subway. Men in bars or diners, men
in the market, market brokers, broken
yet handsome men, cocky escalating
elevator men with scents. All
face the razor
crop of my decapitating
gaze: have I not seen them
as I am – severed like a
Marie Antoinette
on some electronic page?

On sightings
I cut away their bodies and
examine each face avoiding
the blood, the waste, or worse –
bad taste: descending
leathered men wanting nothing
more than to pull themselves
from their sheaths, or men
on leashes.

Only dogs
sway me from my tyranny
for I am an animal
lover. But men in lines
may as well be mug
shots, the authorities and I having read
their implausible self-descriptors. Men
who are comfortable
in jeans or tuxes or sunsets
are most endangered, their vast
numbers no sure thing.

CARWASH

It's a strange thing about me
I always have deep thoughts moving
through a carwash, I think about
the guys, always guys,
looking despite all that water
greasy and neglected
but not beaten, not yet,
like limp cigarettes   coffee break hostages
clamped between a few gray teeth

I try to look blasé
like I am one of them
        and not my car

I try as the slap and shimmy
of their soaped leanness
tentacles to explore my whole body
not to look at their limbs
crisscrossed with filthy rivulets from me
or into their eyes
oily and hooded beneath the soiling monotony
or to wonder if they still dream

so instead I think
about you, how I drove through you
so fast I almost lost
control nearly slid
down your ingenious limbs
into you, nearly got awash

and now
as I emerge once again from the tunnel
of foam, leap momentarily from my vehicle
to let in some limbs to polish
take my cash and then I jump back in,
encased again

I am annoyed at the odour left
of guys and my own
unfathomable misfortunes

THE PATIENT CONSIDERS HER PARTS

It's nice they have diagrams
in doctors' offices
comforting as atlases dividing the sick

and brutal world into just a few
pleasant colours. You feel
like a doctor yourself the way the body parts

knowably, without metaphor to aid it
though I can't help myself. I see
the stomach as fetal

rubber cloud, the humpback liver
sleek and breaching in a sea
of scotch from last night.

Observe the lining of the uterus
thickening, receding, over and over
like it just can't make up its mind.

And those brainy intestines
are soft as a scholar finding real fortitude
elusive, self-hating as the hairless caterpillar

colon who wants nothing more than
metamorphosis – to feel winged
like the lucky lungs above.

The office door opens,
I am exposed as porcelain
vertebrae

shaky as a civilization
once indefatigable,
promising, young.

SECRETS

Once I knew an administrator who
claimed to love my deep structure. But
one day he moved in, hammered,
and tried to renovate.

A step up was the architect,
classically trained, whose soft
dreamy hands climbed silent and
untouching, adulating up my scaffolding.
Modernly, with the dawn, I slipped away.

More recently there was the psychologist,
which could have come in handy, but though
he could name all my thoughts he
possessed far too few of his own.

And that lawyer, well, his tongue
still comes around with free estimates
of his stellar future, inviting me
along for a ride in his firm
pointing lap.

It's hard too
to forget the professor,
whose cleverness flashed blindingly,
as wave tips between sails,
through his mind   body split.

The last was the publisher who wanted to see me in print
sheets with other men, and only if I paid him up front,
and when he asked for a refund, I gave back
him to himself.

Here, in Chapala, Mexico,
where the poverty is general
my secrets do not translate
that well.

AISLE OF HOPE
(a drugstore romance)

Me, I'd just come from Cosmetics where
lips wait, erect, in moist pairs
eyes float alone in spiked dairy stares and
            not far from the starched dry silence
            of Hygiene and the cool hush
            between condoms and the pharmacist
women ask pointed questions.

It was the perfect intersection.
Our wrists brushing
soft as a breeze breathing
over pink tissue roses on a wedding sedan
or the sleek haunches of a Trojan
like the one on that fated box.

As we touched it
together it careened down between our knees
which softened as we rounded
to breathe in the first of each other.

And the pharmacist flushed
as we vaulted, careless, into Haircare.

There, your long thick
reach down my short bolero
saved me as I tried to grip
at a wall of products
but my hand slipped on the viscous ribbons
of cream and amber
spilling from the shelf pressed
hard behind us.

Soon a photocopier
was springing to life as you laid me
across the warm glass

and we copied our copulations
        perfectly, perfectly

and the aisle filled
        with people, hope.

The cerulean night flicked on as he rode in on that look—a melter.
And those thick hands slightly charcoal at the knuckles from cogitation
in the Harley stable, hands of Michelangelo, made her lose
and lose her place in her book. *Kerouac?* she asked
of the volume protruding from his jeans; this so natural, literary
allusion as an opening. His eyes cantered around her, slow and blue
as Ulysses around the nymph's grotto; then he was there, above her
table for one, her glasses limp upon her knee. *Parts Manual,* he replied,
slapping his leather hip with pride. Yet something bolted through her
beauty like a shifted paradigm, and she was helpless when he said,
holding all her sadness and hunger in the palms of his eyes,
Would the lady like a lager?

SONG AT HIDDEN LAKE

I

The sun rises and the roof of ice
above me jazzes with strict
slanted heat. I count crackles
for hours, awaiting spring.
Still, you knew I was down there.

At first, the filaments of grass
stroking themselves like bows is
all I hear. Those reeds, and the small winds
of plankton braiding between my thighs:
my winter symphonic.

It is from there, where the memory of light
at rest on the bottom of the lake looks up
at the puzzle of ice, that you felt me.
From that kind of distance.

II

A long-armed man,
you sent shards of shale singing across
the cold firmament until a piece of ice
broke away. Up I came.

As though the rest
were a dream and you were a tree
and I a magpie.

III

And just as the poplar allows the magpie,
an unlikely aviatory thing, to visit,
and welcomes it like a savant, and the
magpie says *Show me the genius
of your limbs*, we began.

OPENING
New York City

People hang at The Opening; languid, in love
with their black-on-blacks. Mouths parting like small rubber
change-purses, pinched, releasing just enough, accepting
the occasional cube of pale cheese, chocolate-sunk berry, thin lip
of glass.

Through their scrim I see you: inhabiting the space
before a large canvas
of a man in a chair, a bleak shaft of light
pinning him and his disintegrating face
into the corner of a room. But you are smiling

the smile of one who, having had his soul
stolen by a photograph, can now get on with it.
The pain is so complete; the painting has set you free.

Then you are smiling at my dropped program. As though my blouse
had slipped off, drifted to the floor at your feet, smiling as
my heart *wick-wacked* and I did it again.

It is New York City, night streets so ice-bitten even the taxis
are shy.

FEVER

Haunted by the butter you left at the bedside I must
run – take in a film. No use; I come back.
From the mantle I take and rotate a carving,
a soapstone man in the grip of a raven grinning;
round and round in one hand, it's small enough.
I try the tube. Reruns on the History Channel;
history repeating itself. I flip to a film, but it's the same
one I paid for earlier, or may as well
be. Some fetish thing, your
kind of thing. Back in bed I variegate
the covers, dream of big ships unfurling, leaving,
returning with outlandish bounty, news of the new world.
But the butter – still there on the night table. Its oblong
slowness. This empty hand. The incessant night hollow.

Spring

Pleasure is
a noisy neighbour you want
to invite in

even the corridor
is divine. Alone in its cage
my tongue –

the tiger is famished.
Where are you?
My ears press tightly against

my head listening:
for the feral
grain of your voice.

I see your cock
standing up like a
scholar, a rose in its teeth.

What can I? I water I
water you, all my lips
aflutter.

Now my night table
has gone deaf. Come back,
I will run words

through your limbs. Cherry blossoms
are flooding
the avenues, Come.

We'll haul out the boat.
The one with the music
and the mirrors.

BLOOD TEST

Even if our March
never comes, the mean of winter
has not ever been so tender. That has me
in Grade 6, Terence Something
signing my broken leg
with kisses and I am briefly popular.
In other words, glory.

When you and I discussed
marriage and getting all the related tests
on our first date, however, and on the third
I moved in, in other words, doornails
are wiser, a crowd of frantic sentences gathered in me
lonesome and replete as a Mariachi
band in search of anonymity.

All the latrinalia
I've consulted has advised change
and some establishments have
gotten specific. Hillary
or maybe that was Helen
has me considering reconstructive surgery
or maybe that was sodomy
and knowing her
as I do makes me question why
we shouldn't just invite her home
break some legs and drink tequila
till the rabbi and the lab give us a call.

BLUE HERON AMORE

She couldn't help it. That caw
rising from somewhere behind
the spikes of green

fringe around the lagoon
made even me moisten.
She emerged on foot

stepping into our path
until the sound froze
her Giocommetti-like

on the road.
That sound of the other
striking the air, one long

intricate sibilant commanding
Come! up through a snaking throat.
Then her ballerina core, that impossible

skinny lift-off
straight up. It got me inside
my own knees.

The sky parted wide,
detailed with soaring.
Later we discussed flying dreams.

No Light at Dawn

Alone again, my bearded friend.
Locked in. Glass
after glass babbling to you.

Things grin: who.
Are you puzzles & palimpsests –
photos on the hearth?

You two were a pair
of fine cutlery, aimed at different things
on the plate. Now she's off feeding herself

to the ravenous night
while a pock, a hollow
grows where her words fell

like planets into you. When dawn
mercifully arrives, there is less:
sensation, not betrayal.

Eventually
she returns, teeters
on heels outside

near cool morning milk. Fat
and weightless
on smoke and fragrance.

OPTISCHISM

I'm the kind of person who says the glass is half
A buck at the discount place, or
Indelibly kissed – though the dishwasher weeps all day.

My thorns are examining their roses,
Rain is giving my head a bricking, and
I'm the kind of person who says the glass is half

The glass it used to be
Twice as transparent –
The kisses stamped on it insufficient postage.

I can't deny in my garden is written everything
One could imagine, and there are drugs anyway.
So why am I the kind of person who says the glass is half?

It's funny how the days break off a little
Brittle. I had meant to seaside, splash fish
Kisses on our table, weeping aside.

Instead I rained my bric-a-brac
Idiom, the scent from which you guessed
I am the kind of person who says the glass is half

And half and half, forked
And frantic with doubt.

The Truth about Bartleby*

He gazes at her through slats – lines across
early evening's page. As she ascends a hill
he gently spreads the shutters.
Sun is setting, the sky a hysteria.

She had said to him, *I must go*
into this time of night where, look: it is perfect
for consideration.
But he knows it hard
as the ebony studs in her lobes and her violet
eyes that make little pools in his palms
that what she is weighing is love
for another, perhaps someone with letters
after his name.

Skein upon skein of terrifying pinks
and tans fill up the space behind her silk-
worm hair, the mad plaid of her little dress
inside her perfectly lettered silhouette.

He copies it with his eyes:
the bowed I of her length, the *T*
of her arms stroking the lucky breeze,
the sweet lower case *c's*
(if only he were near her, on her, a horizontal *B*)
protruding below her fine, Modigliani neck.

Poor Bartleby!
Later, with her two hands cupped heatless
around his plump and inky ones, his knee
burnished and folded at her feet,
the flat line arrives, and she says:
I would prefer not to.

And the words stamp
into his lonesome tongue.

* *Bartleby is the title character from Herman Melville's short story,* Bartleby, the Scrivner *about an enigmatic clerk whose job it is to make copies of letters, but whose response to orders suddenly and inexplicably becomes "I would prefer not to."*

BIRD

Small brown bird
nesting in my willow

pitches itself over
and over into the window
where I am peering out

learning nothing
over and over

into the window
where I am
learning nothing
over and over.

One of us ought to be flattered.

BIRD 2

Six months later, other birds are hurling
themselves into my window, and a relative is
dead on the back porch. I think of cicadas

who return every seven years
or so and riot to exhaustion among
the boughs and pitted oak.

Their shrill vibrations
ring the world with all
that saved up life

as they gnaw mad, starving,
into green flesh. Leaves
vanish like valentines.

Mistakes are made
of desire. Just as desire
swallowed

our few weeks of heat
whole like Jonah
and we swam

to where the roads are lined
with throngs of light-
headed birds and

the earth is ruby
with pain. Who knew
we were that hungry?

THE GIFT
(a tale of revenge)

I dreamed you telephoned.

Unscrewing the receiver
I bared the works
plunged my fingers
wittingly among the wires
and yanked out plenty
(the static must have
driven you mad)
enough wire to slit
off a lobe
(why squander all
when it's just love
not art
at stake?)
and I laid it tenderly
inside, then tightened the device
so you could hear
my body   part
half way round
the bloody globe.

THE WOOF OF REASON

My mail has developed an attitude.
The bills and notices of rejection
in particular have become quarrelsome;
my hallway is in a bad mood. The cloth nap
of my nightrobe is thickening with sticky kitchen
residue. A dog is something I'm thinking
I might need. Even the extravagant fireworks show
has begun to make sense. And just yesterday
when my mother flushed with the news
she may have the forgetting disease
I forgot my manners and ran away to weep.

I am spending far too much time alone.
Surely, the dog will explain it all to me.

EXIT

My shoes fill
like small shallow lungs,
I am leaving.

The door reaches, takes
me out into the slap
of morning, myself again

as you call out from the shower
something about dinner.

Outside ice branches beneath my feet
capillaries bursting under each step
ending an age.

In the cafes
talk already about the night
before, the ones to come

and in the alley ways,
the odd pair
of frozen feet, hands

that may have loved you
better, or me.

BENEATH

The sky is crinolined and fluted.
Lacey: a feminine anger.
Palms turn upward
feeling. Marry me one
is inclined to say to anyone.
In case this is it, the end of summers.

In case that old Abelard
on the corner, shielding his newspaper
like a love letter inside a big coat,
is the last sentient being.
A promise of showers and war
warming on his ashen languor.

It goes like this more often than I'd like.
A mild grade condition of some sort.
Brain is a weapon of mass
deconstruction. The heart lingers
beneath, doodling away the ache.